POSEIDON

APEX

T0014692

By Christine Ha

WWW.APEXEDITIONS.COM

Apex is distributed by North Star Editions:
sales@northstareditions.com | 888-417-0195

Produced for Apex by Red Line Editorial.

Photographs ©: Shutterstock Images, cover, 1, 4–5, 6–7, 8–9, 10–11, 12–13, 14, 15, 16–17, 18–19, 20–21, 22–23, 24–25, 26, 27, 29

Library of Congress Control Number: 2020952927

ISBN
978-1-63738-016-1 (hardcover)
978-1-63738-052-9 (paperback)
978-1-63738-122-9 (ebook pdf)
978-1-63738-088-8 (hosted ebook)

Printed in the United States of America
Mankato, MN
082021

NOTE TO PARENTS AND EDUCATORS

Apex books are designed to build literacy skills in striving readers. Exciting, high-interest content attracts and holds readers' attention. The text is carefully leveled to allow students to achieve success quickly. Additional features, such as bolded glossary words for difficult terms, help build comprehension.

TABLE OF CONTENTS

CHAPTER 1

ROUGH WATERS

A ship sailed along the coast. It was about to begin a long journey. Suddenly, Poseidon appeared. He swung his **trident**. Dark clouds filled the sky.

Poseidon is often shown holding a trident. He used this weapon to control the sea.

Greek ships could have both oars and sails. The sails caught the wind.

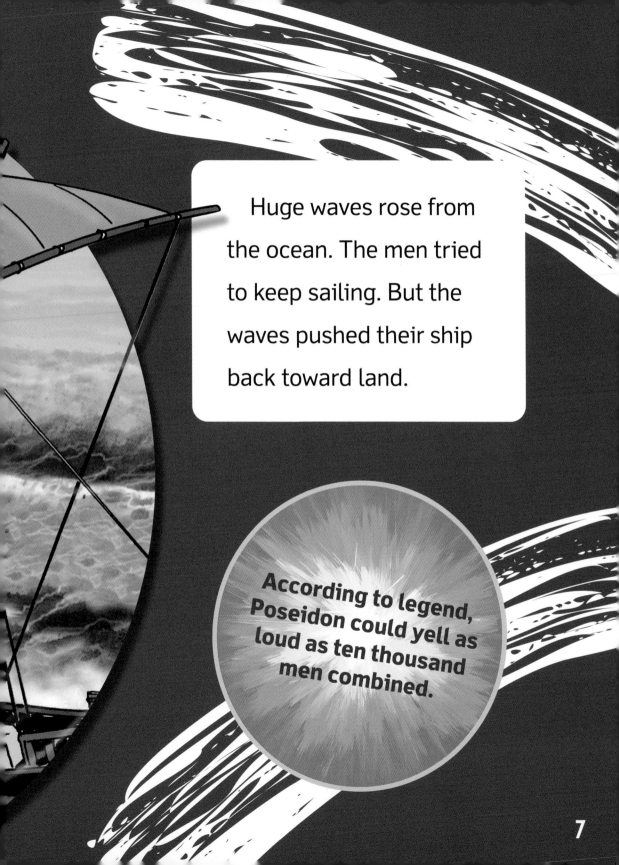

Huge waves rose from the ocean. The men tried to keep sailing. But the waves pushed their ship back toward land.

According to legend, Poseidon could yell as loud as ten thousand men combined.

Poseidon **vanished**. But the waves were still too dangerous. The men hoped the god would be in a better mood tomorrow.

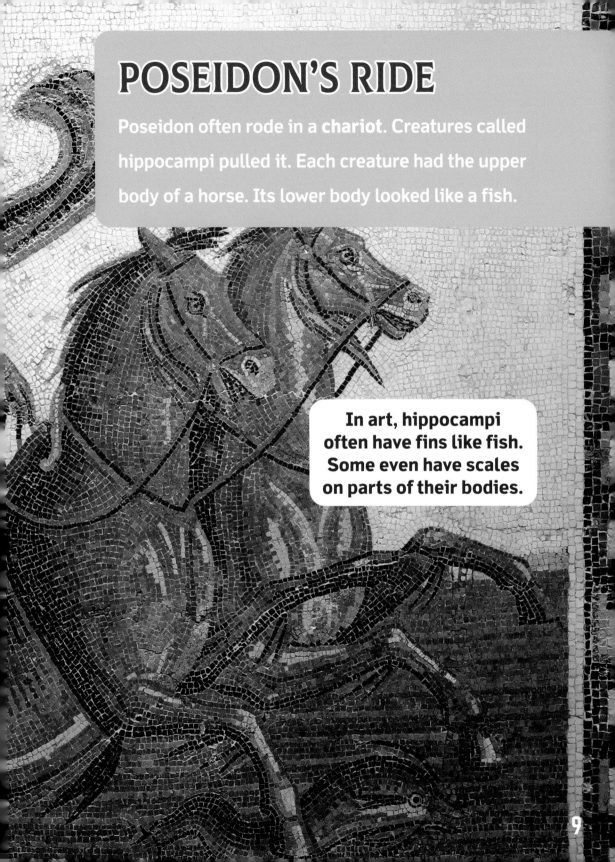

POSEIDON'S RIDE

Poseidon often rode in a **chariot**. Creatures called hippocampi pulled it. Each creature had the upper body of a horse. Its lower body looked like a fish.

In art, hippocampi often have fins like fish. Some even have scales on parts of their bodies.

CHAPTER 2

WATER GOD

Poseidon was the Greek god of the sea. He could cause storms, floods, and earthquakes.

Poseidon caused earthquakes by striking his trident against the ground.

Statues of sea nymphs often decorate fountains.

Poseidon lived at the bottom of the sea. He had a beautiful palace there. It was made of gems and coral.

Legends say many nymphs lived in the ocean. One became Poseidon's wife. Her name was Amphitrite.

Poseidon protected sailors who traveled by sea. He guided their ships to safety. But if he got angry, he could send waves or storms.

Poseidon had many children. Some were monsters or sea creatures.

Legends say Poseidon was the father of the winged horse, Pegasus.

Triton was one of Poseidon's sons. He had the tail of a fish.

LORD OF HORSES

Poseidon was also the god of horses. Stories said he created the first horse. He struck his trident against a rock. A horse jumped out.

CHAPTER 3

OFTEN ANGRY

Like the waters he ruled, Poseidon was unpredictable. He got angry easily. And he could be **vengeful**.

Poseidon caused lots of problems for people he didn't like.

Once, Poseidon helped build walls around a city. The city's king didn't want to pay him. Poseidon got very angry.

When Poseidon got angry, he sometimes sent sea monsters to attack people.

In one story, a hero blinded Poseidon's son. Poseidon made the hero stay lost at sea for 10 years.

Cetus is a constellation in the night sky. This group of stars is named after a sea monster Poseidon sent to attack people.

He sent a sea monster to attack the city. It grabbed people who came near the shore. But a hero killed it.

ANOTHER ATTACK

In one story, a queen bragged that her daughter was prettier than all the sea nymphs. Poseidon got mad. He sent a sea monster to kill the daughter. A hero saved her.

CHAPTER 4

POSEIDON'S TEMPLES

Poseidon was popular throughout Greece. But he was especially important along the coasts. Many of his temples were near bodies of water.

Greece has almost 8,500 miles (13,700 km) of coastline.

Part of Poseidon's temple at Cape Sounion still stands today.

For example, one famous temple was built on **Cape** Sounion. Another stood on the **Isthmus** of Corinth. This area was part of a major trade route. From there, ships sailed around the world.

POSEIDON'S CITY

Poseidon was the **patron** of Corinth. Every two years, the city held a **festival** in his honor. It featured music and sports. There were horse races as well.

In Rome, Poseidon was known by the name Neptune.

At temples, people made **offerings** to Poseidon. They asked for safe travels. And they requested help with fishing and trade.

Sea bass was one type of fish that people caught in ancient Greece.

Some places held boat races to honor Poseidon.

COMPREHENSION QUESTIONS

Write your answers on a separate piece of paper.

1. Write a few sentences describing the main ideas of Chapter 2.

2. Would you rather have the power to cause earthquakes or to create storms? Why?

3. Which creatures pulled Poseidon's chariot?

   A. fish

   B. nymphs

   C. hippocampi

4. Why were Poseidon's temples built near water?

   A. Most of Poseidon's powers involved water.

   B. Poseidon disliked water and avoided it.

   C. Poseidon had no powers on land.

5. What does **unpredictable** mean in this book?

*Like the waters he ruled, Poseidon was **unpredictable**. He got angry easily.*

    A. never getting angry

    B. always staying calm

    C. often changing moods

6. What does **requested** mean in this book?

*They asked for safe travels. And they **requested** help with fishing and trade.*

    A. stood next to something

    B. asked for something

    C. fell off something

Answer key on page 32.

GLOSSARY

cape
A narrow area of land that sticks out into a body of water.

chariot
A two-wheeled cart pulled by horses or other animals.

festival
A day or time of celebration, often based on a religion.

isthmus
A thin strip of land that connects two large areas of land.

nymphs
Beautiful spirits that live in trees, water, or other parts of nature.

offerings
Gifts to a god or goddess to get his or her help or favor.

patron
A person who gives help or support.

trident
A spear with three points.

vanished
Left quickly without a trace.

vengeful
Wanting to hurt someone who has hurt you.

TO LEARN MORE

BOOKS

Bell, Samantha S. *Ancient Greece.* Lake Elmo, MN: Focus Readers, 2020.

Buckey, A. W. *Greek Gods, Heroes, and Mythology.* Minneapolis: Abdo Publishing, 2019.

Temple, Teri. *Poseidon: God of the Sea and Earthquakes.* Mankato, MN: The Child's World, 2019.

ONLINE RESOURCES

Visit **www.apexeditions.com** to find links and resources related to this title.

ABOUT THE AUTHOR

Christine Ha lives in Minnesota. She enjoys reading and learning about myths and legends from around the world.

INDEX

Answer Key:
1. Answers will vary; **2.** Answers will vary; **3.** C; **4.** A; **5.** C; **6.** B